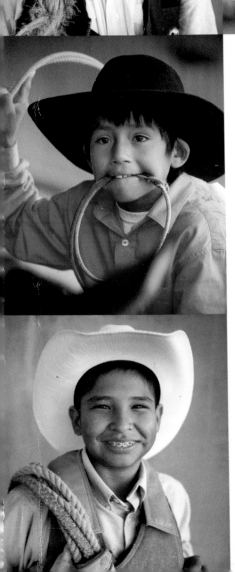

Rodeo Rider

I want to be a rodeo rider—
a barrel racing,
        crazy bull chasing,
lasso slinging,
        wild calf roping,
bronco busting,
        mutton tumbling,
rodeo rider.

COWBOY UP!
RIDE THE NAVAJO RODEO

NANCY BO FLOOD  PHOTOGRAPHY BY **JAN SONNENMAIR**

WORDSONG
AN IMPRINT OF HIGHLIGHTS
Honesdale, Pennsylvania

Acknowledgements

A sincere round of applause and gratitude to
Frank Young, Rob Taylor, Lita Manygoats, Joey
Sells Hanley, and all the other rodeo mentors
who work day jobs, then spend evenings and
weekends teaching kids of all ages the skills of
riding and roping. These dedicated volunteers
foster the can-do attitudes of confidence and
kindness needed in any arena: Help your fellow
rider. Respect all critters, including two-legged
ones. Falling off is the first part of learning. The
second part is getting up, climbing back on, and
trying again.

  Thank you also to Marcia Leonard, editor
of *Cowboy Up!*, and to Mary-Alice Moore, who
believed in the project from day one.

Tough enough to wear pink. Many of the
rodeo competitors and audience members
photographed for this book are wearing pink
in honor of breast cancer awareness.

Text copyright © 2013 by Nancy Bo Flood
Photographs copyright © 2013 by Jan Sonnenmair

WORDꟅONG

An Imprint of Highlights
815 Church Street
Honesdale, Pennsylvania 18431
Printed in Mexico

ISBN: 978-1-59078-893-6
Library of Congress Control Number: 2012949009
First edition

10 9 8 7 6 5 4 3 2 1

To Julie Larios, word wrangler, poetry queen.
—*NBF*

In memory of my beautiful mother, Gloria, and for my son, Eli, the finest buckaroo to travel with on the dusty trail.
—*JS*

Tomorrow

Can't eat.
Can't sleep.
Mind keeps figuring, figuring, figuring—
how tight to hold,
how far to lean,
how hard to squeeze
to stay on top.
Cowboy up!
Rodeo tomorrow.

Love My Lariat

I sure do love my lariat
like my horse loves sweet oats,
like my dog loves a belly rub,
like my little brother loves climbing fences.
I sure do love hearing
my lariat sing,
feeling it spin
till it snags
that long-horned steer,
that big-eyed calf,
that lop-eared goat—
or my backyard practice bull.

Just as many Little League baseball players dream of competing in the World Series, many young Navajo ropers and riders dream of competing in the National Finals Rodeo. Most evenings after school, these young wranglers practice riding or lassoing, spinning a lariat over a pair of horns fixed to a sawhorse or a bale of hay. Rodeo riders are honored athletes—skilled, smart, and tough. It takes brains, muscles, and a lot of practice to wrestle a racing steer to the ground or stay on top of a bucking, twisting bronco. Rodeo is the number-one most exciting sport out West. Not so sure? Take a look. Let's rodeo!

Gathering

I think about that empty arena,
the first morning light
making golden shafts in the sleepy dust
as stockmen's trucks rumble down the gravel road.
Soon they'll unload
mean-looking steers,
bulls and broncos,
sheep and goats,
and nervous calves,
legs trembling as they scramble down the trailer ramp,
wondering,
What happens next?

 rodeo arena is a part of nearly every Navajo community—even though that community might count more horses than people, certainly more cattle or sheep than children. The arena is basically a fence surrounding a dusty stretch of dirt and sand, the whole area about the size of a baseball diamond. Along the middle of one side is a tall wooden stand, the official perch for the rodeo announcer. All day long he'll call out the events, give the winning times, tell a few tales, and play twangy country-western music. Bleachers flank the other side of the arena. Corrals run along the ends, pens for keeping rough stock: Brahma bulls, broncos, and sheep for riding, calves and steers for roping. An arena isn't much to look at when it's empty. But on rodeo days, it's full of life and excitement.

9

That's My Grandpa

Your silver buckle says World Champion Saddle Bronc Rider,
right, Grandpa?

    I reckon so.

You were all-around national champion,
right, Grandpa?

    Yep.

Riding broncos, bulldogging steers, roping runaway calves—
better and faster than anyone. Right, Grandpa?

    Horse and rider, we were a working team.

Now you're the best rodeo announcer in the whole wide West.

    Maybe so.

Rodeo is in me, too, Grandpa. Beating in my heart.

    Seems to be.

Me and my horse will race round those barrels,
maybe make all-around peewee champion!

    Could happen. Soon as you stop your jabbering and start riding.
    Think you're ready?

I reckon so.

rucks pulling horse trailers arrive early in the morning at the rodeo grounds. As soon as one's backed into its proper place, people pop out and start unloading horses. They brush them down, braid their tails and manes, and generally shine them up like they were getting ready for a beauty contest. But don't let the spit and polish fool you. These horses are tough!

Navajo rodeo is a family affair. Grandma in her turquoise jewelry and velvet skirt watches from the stands. An infant is rocked by one young cousin before being passed to another. The youngest cowpokes strut around in their spanking-clean cowboy shirts and jeans, twirling peewee lariats. And older competitors think about making that perfect throw or holding on for the perfect ride to win that big silver buckle: "Champion." Everyone in the family participates.

Grand Entry

Shoulder to shoulder, flank to flank,
horses and riders gallop out.
They circle round
making fancy formations,
then stop,
wait for the honor guard to carry in the colors.
The crowd stands up,
quiets.
Hats come off.
Heads are bowed
to show respect for the national anthem
and the "Cowboy's Prayer":
> Make me as big and open as the plains,
> As honest as the horse between my knees,
> Clean as the wind that blows behind the rains,
> Free as the hawk that circles down the breeze!

A burst of applause, the arena empties,
and before the red dust settles or the rainbow fades,
we hear loud and clear—

Everyone please take your seats!
Ladies and gents, give a big warm welcome to our youngest competitors. First call, all you peewee cowpokes. Mutton-bustin' woolly-sheep wranglers, get ready to ride.

Woolly Rider

Sit on top—
sheep's kicking mad—
fingers curled tight,
one hand held high.
Ready . . . set . . .
Ya-a-a-hooo!

1 second	We're flying! Whole world blurs by.
2 seconds	Stomach up my throat. Crowd cheers. I'm holding on.
3 seconds	Sheep swerves. Oops, sliding off. Yank back up.
4 seconds	Hand hurts. Need to pee.
5 seconds	Fingers numb. Eyes shut. Still on.
6 seconds	Arms ache. Knees shake. Legs squeeze.
7 seconds	Sheep bucks. Starts to roll. Slipping, sliding. Gotta hold . . . gotta hold . . .
8 seconds	On!

Roll off, stand up, crowd cheers.
I grin.
Yes, sirree, I'm a mutton-bustin' woolly rider, me!

o be a woolly rider, a boy or girl must be at least four years old and weigh not an ounce over fifty pounds. The rider sits on top of a full-grown sheep confined to a narrow chute. One hand holds on to a leather strap. The other hand is held high and must never touch the animal.

Once the sheep leaps out the chute, the rider tries to stay on its back for eight long seconds. But the sheep wants that rider off, so it tries all sorts of tricks. A sheep might take off so fast the rider is left behind, sitting in the dust. It might flop onto its stomach or roll over. It might skid to a sudden stop, sending the rider sailing over its head.

Most riders tumble off in the first few seconds. But these tough cowpokes stand up, fight back tears, spit out a mouthful of dirt—and march out of the arena grinning as the crowd cheers.

Bronc Riders

Riders are standing by.

Horses are in the chutes. We have
some of the roughest, toughest
wranglers and best-ranked broncs.
So set your hands clapping, give 'em
plenty of encouragement.
Next competitor, ready to ride.
Cowboy up!

No saddle or stirrups.
 Are you crazy?
 Got my lucky saddle hitched tight.
Nothing to hold on to
but a braided rawhide rigging.
 Got my reins held right.
Ready!
 Ready!
Out the chute.
 Heels pressed in.
One hand held high.
 Feeling the rhythm of a
kicking,
 rearing,
twisting,
 spinning

BRONC!

Bareback rider,
 Saddleback rider,

YEAH!

he rules for bareback and saddle-bronc riding are short and tough: The rider holds on with one hand and waves the other hand high overhead, fighting for balance. And when coming out the chute, the rider's spurs must be touching the horse clear up past its shoulders. Riding gear is different for the two events. A bareback rider only has a twisted rope to hold on to. A saddle-bronc rider sits on a modified saddle and uses reins and stirrups.

A perfect score is one hundred points, half based on the horse's performance and half on the rider's. The more bucking, twisting, rearing, and spinning the horse does, the higher its rank. A "legal ride" requires staying on for a full eight seconds—six if the rider, boy or girl, is a junior competitor. If the rider flies off before the buzzer, he or she receives no score, no credit. The ride is DQ, disqualified.

Calf Roper

Ladies and gents,

all eyes to the arena for our first timed event. Watch close, or you just might miss the action. These calf ropers are fast as lightning!

I sit my horse low,
piggin' string between my teeth,
reins in my left hand, lariat in my right.
I watch
from one stall
as the wide-eyed calf
waits in the other.

"Raise the gate!"
Out leaps that doggie!
Horse reaching,
calf racing,
seconds ticking,
rope twirling.

My lasso
strikes like a snake.
I spin my horse back,
set my rope tight.
Leap off,
tie that calf's legs.
Done!

Yep, a mighty fine run.

Calf roping is one of the oldest events in rodeo. It dates back to the days when cattle were raised on the open range, and a cowboy's job included chasing and lassoing calves and steers for branding, sorting, and doctoring.

Both girls and boys compete in this event, starting as young as eight years old. Catching a calf on the run demands quick reflexes, skill, strength, and speed of both horse and rider. A competitor must lasso the calf, flip it onto the ground, tie three of its legs together using a rope called a piggin' string, and then throw both hands up to signal "done!" The struggling calf must stay tied for five seconds before kicking free, or it's a DQ. Times are competitive down to one hundredth of a second.

Barrel Racer

Next timed event:
barrel racing! Get ready to watch some fast-turning horses and riders. Let's have a big round of applause for our first cowgirl, ready to fly around the barrels.

The bleachers are packed full.
Everyone's watching.
What if I fall?
What if my time is too slow?
One more rider, then
me.

"Next rider up!"
I click my tongue,
push my boots hard in the stirrups,
heels down.
My hands are sweaty,
but I hold the reins right.
Ready, girl.
Ride!

I bust through the gate,
spin round the first barrel,
shoot to the second
and circle around tight,
leaning so hard, my stirrup kicks dirt.
Streak to the last barrel—
spin, fly, race down the middle.
Home!

arrel racing is all about speed and balance. The barrels are set up in a three-leaf clover pattern, one barrel at each point. Horse and rider race out of the gate and spin around the first barrel, leaning so hard to the right that spurs scrape dirt. The rider shifts her weight to straighten out the horse. Then they race to the next barrel, circling around it leaning left this time. After racing around the third and final barrel, horse and rider gallop straight back home to the starting point. The rider with the fastest time—usually just under fourteen seconds—wins the event. At the senior level, only women riders, often called lady girls, compete.

Midway Walk

Are you cowpokes getting hungry?

There's plenty of fine food waiting on the midway. Your nose will lead you to mutton stew, juicy barbecue ribs, or a plate-size piece of fry bread. Wash it all down with some ice-cold pop. Then visit our fine vendors. Just remember to come on back to watch the best in the West in the second half of our show.

Wearing my new boots
    steel-toed, stay-in-the-stirrup
    saddle-bronc boots.
Sporting my new hat
    wide-brimmed, keep-off-the-sun
    wrangler hat.
Slapping my new chaps
    low-slung, fringe-at-the-sides
    bull-riding chaps.
I'll be struttin' the midway.

Midway Eats

Hey, what's this?
I sashay back,
nose sniffing,
stomach growling.
Going to buy me some
crisp, hot fry bread,
grease still popping, sweet honey
oozing,
curly fries and a big, juicy burger,
hot chili peppers heaped on top.
Wash it all down with
thirst-quenching, head-numbing,
blue shaved ice.
Oh, yeah! Mighty fine.

Steer Wrestler

Ladies and gents,
time to get back to business.
I guarantee you've had enough to
eat—plus a mouthful of dust and a
heaping portion of hot sun. Plenty
for your money! So take your seats.
We got some Cadillac cowboys
ready to try their luck wrestling
down racing steers. Let's give our
applause and our attention to this
next rough-stock event.

A fast chase
on a racing horse
catches me up to that mean running steer.
I lean, lean, lean,
get positioned just right,
then split-second leap
on top his shoulders,
hold on to his horns,
crank his neck around
to twist him
down,
then hold that fighting thousand pounds
flat
against the ground.

Steer wrestling.
It takes a real rough, tough wrangler.
Like Bill Pickett.
Like me.

**S**teer wrestling, first called bulldogging, was invented by Bill Pickett, a tough, top-hand cowboy of Cherokee and African American descent. Seems that when Bill was a kid, he saw thirty-pound cow dogs subdue thousand-pound steers by biting them on the lip. So when he traveled with a Wild West show as an adult, that's what *he* did.

He'd throw a bucking bull to the ground with his bare hands and then keep it there by sinking his teeth into the bull's lip. No rope tying needed! As the event became popular on the rodeo circuit, the lip biting ended, but the nickname remained. Bill Pickett was inducted into the National Rodeo Hall of Fame in 1971 and the ProRodeo Hall of Fame in 1989.

Team Roper

Okay, folks,
get yourselves ready for a real
treat! There's nothing finer to
watch than the fast, smooth
action of team roping. So here,
ready to show off their skills, are
some of rodeo's best headers
and heelers.

I started roping when I was barely three,
lassoing fence posts,
goats,
my little brother
till Gramps made me a backyard bull
out of PVC pipe
with handle-bar horns.

When I was in grade school,
most evenings after homework and chores,
I'd get my lariat spinning,
lassoing
head or heels of a race-away sheep.

Now I'm finally tall enough,
strong enough,
good enough
to stay on top a galloping horse,
throw a lasso,
catch a calf.

With Dad as the header,
me as the heeler,
working together
we're a winning team.

eam roping is a popular event because it's a showcase for skilled riding and roping. The first roper, the header, lassos the front of the steer, usually the horns. (The steer wears protective wraps around its horns to prevent rope burns and reduce the risk of a horn breaking.) The second roper, the heeler, snags the steer by its hind feet. (A five-second penalty is added to the end time if only one leg is caught.) Both ropers pull their lariats taut and wrap, or dally, them around their saddle horns so the steer is held tight. Team roping is the only rodeo event in which both men and women compete.

27

Bareback Bull Rider

Finally, folks,

*what we've all been wanting
to watch: bareback bull riding.
We've got some great bulls—
top ranked—and some great
riders. I guarantee it's been worth
your wait. Let's give a great big
encouraging welcome to rodeo's
toughest, strongest, and craziest
competitors. Make no mistake.
This is a dangerous event. The
ambulance folks are standing by.*

Big Brahma bull
stands square,
glares.

Big Brahma bull,
head down,
horns able
to rip a rider wide apart.

Big Brahma bull,
hooves scraping dirt,
blocks of muscle
waiting to explode
out the chute.

Big Brahma bull.
My turn to ride.

ull riding is rodeo's most dangerous event. A Brahma bull is two thousand pounds of fight, and to win, a rider must stay on its back for a full eight seconds. As in bronco riding, the contestant holds one hand high. With his other hand he grips a leather strap that encircles the bull's chest. Riders often cinch the strap so tight there's no chance of accidentally letting go, knowing they run the risk of having fingers broken or pulled out of joint.

Riding a bull to the bell—the eight-second mark—is harder than riding a bronco. Not only does a bull twist, turn, buck, hook, and spin, but its loose skin slips and slides. That makes holding on one-handed particularly difficult.

Hall of Fame rodeo champ Earl Bascom offered this advice: for bull-riding practice, start your day riding a wild steer bareback and backwards.

Big, Bad Bulls

Just a reminder, folks,

while you're watching our top-ranked bulls tonight: the two bulls considered the deadliest in rodeo history were Bodacious and Tornado—both known for being nearly impossible to ride and for charging at fallen riders.

Bodacious was a bad bucking bull,
ranked the toughest in all the West,
in all the world.
I'm not bragging, lying, or exaggerating.
More than a hundred top wranglers tried to ride him.
Not even ten stayed on for the full eight-second count.
Some barely survived.

Bodacious,
the orneriest, deadliest,
twisting, spinning, kicking, leaping
bull
ever.

Bulls are ranked or scored on how tough they are to ride. Cowboys hope to draw a top-ranked animal, even though the "opportunity" might be deadly. Bodacious was the first bull inducted into the ProRodeo Hall of Fame. Some of the other famous bulls in rodeo history include the aptly named Scorpion, Cyclone, Dead-On-Arrival and Black Widow.

The highest score ever given in this rough-stock event was a perfect 100. It was earned in 1991 by Wade Leslie, who rode a bull named Wolfman.

Matador of the Rodeo

Before we conclude
*our show this evening, let's give
a special round of applause to
those crazy, clowning-around
bullfighters. They may be funny
looking, but they risk their lives
to keep our competitors safe.*

I shake my floppy hat
at the snorting, kicking wall of Brahma bull.
Catch me,
not that fallen rider.
Get me,
bull-fighter, matador, clown.

See my wide red lips,
white face,
too-big pants, looks like I'll trip?
Folks in the bleachers begin laughing
while a rider runs from death.

I wear a silly grin
but never take my eyes off
wrangler or animal.
Watch out—
rider down!
I wag my rear.
Hey, chase me!
Not that hurtin' cowboy.
I dance before danger,
clowning and teasing until
the rider gets back up,
limps away,
safe.

**K**eep an eye on those rodeo bullfighters. They may look like clowns having fun, but don't be fooled. At every rodeo, large or small, they risk their necks to protect the rough-stock competitors, from the youngest woolly rider to the most experienced bull wrangler. Most bullfighters were rodeo champions in their younger days. They understand the animals, the risk of getting gored, kicked, or trampled. Watch closely and you'll see their skill and courage as they keep themselves between a fallen competitor and an angry animal—sheep, bronco, or bull. It's for good reason they are given the highest respect by the rodeo community.

Happy Trails

We're roping this event in, folks.

One last time, put your hands together to show your appreciation for the people behind the scenes and chutes, the stock handlers, the ambulance crew, and all the timers, judges, and officials who make rodeo possible. Travel home safely! Hope to see you at next week's rodeo. Meanwhile, good riding wherever you wander, and happy trails!

nce again the dusty arena is empty, and long, still shadows stretch across the pens and corrals. Stockmen have checked their livestock for injuries, fed and watered them, and loaded them into their trucks. Dust devils swirl down the deserted midway. Food sellers are gone. Vendors have packed up their wares—the saddles and bridles, the western shirts with shiny mother-of-pearl buttons, the lariats, chaps, and boots. All is quiet except for a few empty pop cans tumbling down the bleachers and the rattle of wheels as the last of the families pack their pickup trucks and drive away. Some wranglers are bringing home trophies. Some are returning empty-handed.

Heading Home

Seems everyone is heading home
sporting a champion buckle,
a first-place ribbon,
a mighty happy face.
Not me.

"Losing is part of rodeo.
Falling is how you learn," says Dad.
"Next rodeo is coming right up.
Another chance to ride your best."

Back home,
not hungry,
stomach's like a stone.
"Come sit outside a spell," invites Dad.
"Sky's clear. There's a bucket of stars."

Across the backbone of night,
a streak of light blazes.
"See? Even stars take a tumble," Dad says.

I stare at that wide stretch of sky.
Gets me thinking—
some riders fall off,
some get bucked off,
land hard, face in the dirt,
get scared,
give up.
Not me.

Rodeo History

There's a heap of disagreement about where the first true rodeo took place. Arizona cowboys brag of having hosted the first rodeo in Prescott in 1888. Rodeo events included bronc riding and wild-steer wrestling, and there were judges, prizes, and a paying audience. Texans argue that the first real rodeo was held in Pecos five years earlier, although no admission was charged. Everyone agrees that once rodeos got started, they quickly became popular. The hard-working, cow-punching, longhorn-trail-riding cowboys of the Wild West took pride in showing off their skills. Wranglers of all races, from Canada to Mexico, put on a great show, lassoing runaway calves, wrestling wild steers, and riding bucking broncs.

Today, rodeo is more popular than ever, and many organizations—professional and amateur, national and international—have formed to support it. The season begins in early spring, runs through the summer, and ends in the fall. Wranglers who have accumulated enough points to qualify, compete in the season's final national and international rodeo championships in September.

If you want to experience a pro rodeo, you have plenty to choose from. The Professional Rodeo Cowboys Association sanctions more than eight hundred. Try the Calgary Stampede in Alberta, Canada, Jubilee Days in Laramie, Wyoming, or the Pendleton Round-Up in Oregon. Or visit the National Rodeo Finals, the Super Bowl of rodeo, held every year in Las Vegas. Big time, big money.

If you want to see down-home grass-roots rodeo, visit the Navajo Nation. There's a rodeo event—or several—going on every weekend during the season, and every weekday, families gather in backyard arenas. Three-year-olds strut around with lariats aiming to lasso a practice bull, a live goat, or each other. Five-year-olds learn riding skills atop a sheep or a gentle horse. Older brothers and sisters practice barrel racing or calf roping, helping each other, teasing each other, training their horses. For rodeo competitors, as for every athlete, daily practice means developing strength and skill while gaining patience, confidence, and courage.

Rodeo is not only about riding and roping. It's about caring for the rodeo animals, from the smallest woolly sheep to the biggest Brahma bull. Navajo competitors young and old have a deep love for their horses and respect for rodeo stock and are careful to keep them healthy and fit.

Cowboy up! Time to rodeo.

Resources

Books about Rodeos and the Cowboy Life

Gordon, Ginger. *Anthony Reynoso: Born to Rope*. New York: Clarion Books, 1996.

Harrison, David L. *Cowboys: Voices in the Western Wind*. Illustrated by Dan Burr. Honesdale, PA: WordSong, 2012.

Johnson, Neil. *Jack Creek Cowboy*. New York: Dial Press, 1993.

Johnson, Robin. *Rodeo*. New York: Crabtree Publishing Company, 2010.

Lester, Julius. *Black Cowboy, Wild Horses: A True Story*. Illustrated by Jerry Pinkney. New York: Dial Press, 1998.

Pinkney, Andrea Davis. *Bill Pickett: Rodeo-Ridin' Cowboy*. Illustrated by Brian Pinkney. Orlando, FL: Harcourt Brace & Company, 1996.

Robbins, Ken. *Rodeo*. New York: Henry Holt & Company, 1996.

Stone, Lynn M. All About the Rodeo series. Vero Beach, FL: Rourke Publishing, 2009.

World of Rodeo series. Various authors. New York: Rosen Publishing Group, 2006.

Websites of Native American Rodeo Associations

www.aircarodeo.com.
The All Indian Rodeo Cowboys Association, Inc.

www.cnrarodeo.com.
Central Navajo Rodeo Association

www.nnrca.org.
Navajo Nation Rodeo Cowboys Association

Other Websites of Interest

www.cs.calgarystampede.com.
Calgary Stampede, Calgary, Alberta, Canada

www.cowboysofcolorrodeo.com.
Cowboys of Color Rodeo

www.laramiejubileedays.net.
Laramie Jubilee Days, Laramie, Wyoming

www.nationalcowboymuseum.org.
The National Cowboy & Western Heritage Museum

www.nhsra.com.
National High School Rodeo Association

www.nlbra.com.
National Little Britches Rodeo Association

www.pendletonroundup.com.
Pendleton Roundup, Pendleton, Oregon

www.prorodeo.com.
Professional Rodeo Cowboys Association

www.wpra.com.
Women's Professional Rodeo Association

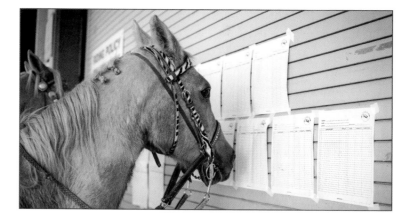

Rodeo Rider

I want to be a rodeo rider—
a barrel racing,
     crazy bull chasing,
lasso slinging,
     wild calf roping,
bronco busting,
     mutton tumbling,
rodeo rider.